Gu
O:

Text: Salvador Sala
Text revised by: Thorsten Meidell and Heinz-Georg Windingstad
(February 2003)

The following photographers employed by Normanns Kunstforlag AS
has contributed: Trygve Gulbrandsen, Giulio Bolognesi,
H. Czochake, Siro Leonardi, Inge Stikholmen, Per Andersen,
Dino Sassi, Kjell Narvestad, Trond Aalde and Terje Bakke Pettersen.

Freelance photographers and institutions contributing:
Espen Bratlie, Fjellanger Widerøe AS, Oslo Bymuseum represented
by Rune Aakvik, Scanpix, Jiri Havran, Nasjonalgaleriet,
Postmuseet, Arkitektmuseet represented by Are Carlsen,
Oslo Sporveier, Samtidsmuseet, Astrup Fernely Museet, Guri Dahl,
Ibsen Museet, Den Norske Husflid, Bård Gudim, Seafood.no,
Den Norske Opera, Stenersenmuseet.

Sales: © **Normanns Kunstforlag AS**
P. o. box 223, N-2001 Lillestrøm
Telf: +47 64802700 Fax: +47 64802701
www.normanns.no - E-mail: normanns@normanns.no

⬦ ESCUDO DE ORO

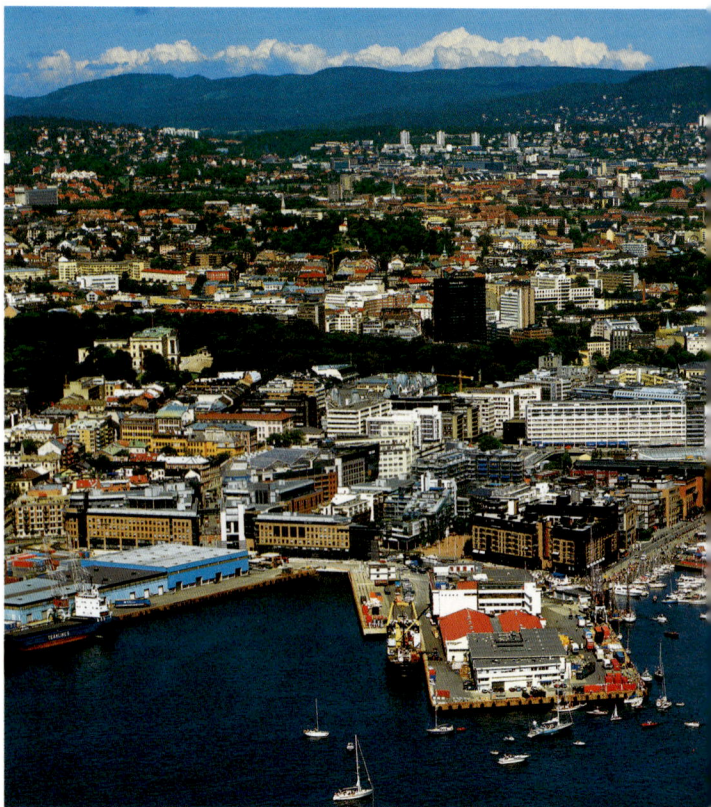

Aerial view of the centre of Oslo.

YOUR VISIT TO OSLO

Oslo has so much to offer: spacious parks, welcoming pedestrianised streets, museums, galleries, the opportunity to practise sport in the surrounding area.... Everything in Oslo is accessible - moving around whether by public transport or organised tour or simply on foot couldn't be easier. Of all the Scandinavian capitals Oslo is perhaps the most convenient for the visitor on foot.

This guide is designed to help you get the most out of your stay in the Viking capital, and it offers you the information that we feel is essential if you are to get a good overall picture of the city. After a brief introduction to the geography and history of the city we go on to suggest five itineraries, each with an introductory map to orientate you when you are exploring the various points of interest described. The first of these itineraries takes you all the way down Karl Johan street from the Royal

Palace to the Central Railway Station, and includes some of the most emblematic buildings of the city in the area, such as the City Hall. In the second we pay a visit to the seafaring side of Oslo, starting at the Akershus fortress and ending up at Aker Brygge. The third itinerary explores the Bygdøy peninsula and the interesting museums to be found there. In the fourth itinerary we take an exclusive look at one of the most fascinating features of the city, Vigeland Park. And in the fifth we take the Munch Museum as our central point.

The guide ends with a chapter on the area round Oslo taking in points of special interest like the Holmenkollen ski jump, and also includes a section with useful advice for the visitor on things like how to get to Oslo, the climate, shopping, prices, eating, entertainment, popular festivals, and how to organise your visit. On the inside covers of the guide you will find plans of the city and the metro.

Oslo from Ekeberg.

OSLO, THE VIKING CAPITAL

The Viking capital of Oslo sits right at the end of the fjord of the same name, 104 km inland from the Skagerak (the sea lying between Norway, Sweden and Denmark), and at the same latitude as Saint Petersburg (Russia) and Anchorage (Alaska). It covers an area of 454 km², of which 295 km² are woods and 23 km² parkland. Its centre is in the shady depths of Nordmarka (Blank-tvannsbråten), a magnificent wood, hikers' paradise in summer and every skier's dream in winter. Perhaps this is why the city was christened Oslo, which in the old Viking tongue means "the grove of the gods".

Oslo, capital of the kingdom of Norway, has more than 500,000 inhabitants, and counting the surrounding areas as well almost reaches the million mark. Approximately one third of the country's population is concentrated within a radius of 100 km around the city. Here are the royal residence and Parliament. The city is also home to an Episcopal see and a University.

The port of Oslo has 13 kilometres of docks, through which most of the country's imports and exports flow. The city itself reflects some of the spectacular economic changes the country has experienced over the last few decades. Predominantly an indus-

4

Vigeland Park.

Hotel Radisson SAS.

trial centre until the 50s, it has since been transformed into a cosmopolitan, active and international capital city. The glass tower of the Hotel Plaza Radisson SAS, at 113 m the highest building in Norway, and the Aker Brygge dock have become the new twin symbols of this oldest city in Scandinavia, with more than 1,000 years of history behind it.

Some 7,000 years ago the earliest-known inhabitants of Oslo settled on the banks of the fjord at Ekeberg Hill and a market gradually grew up on this fertile and secure land. The Viking King Harald Hardråde is attributed with the honour of founding the city here. Although Bergen was the country's first capital, the centre of commercial and military control gradually began to drift eastwards, so that when Håkon V came to the throne in 1299 he transferred the capital of his kingdom from Bergen to Oslo, building the fortress of Akershus to protect his new capital. However, a series of fires, the plague and the unions with Sweden and later Denmark held back the later development of the city. In 1624 Oslo was destroyed by yet

Sculpture of King Christian IV.

another fire. King Christian IV then ordered its reconstruction around the Akershus fortress, and he changed its name to Christiania, a name it retained until 1925.

1814 saw Norway entering a union with Sweden. At the time, Christiania at it was still known was a small city with barely 15,000 inhabitants. But its new distinction as the country's capital - previously everything had been decided from Copenhagen - demanded the construction of some key public buildings – the Stock exchange, the Bank of Norway, the Royal Palace, the University and Parliament. Gradually Karl Johan Avenue (formerly Slottsveien – the path of the Palace) became the new city centre, stretching from the Royal Palace to Eger Square, later known as Jernbanestasjonen (Railway station). The whole avenue was soon lined with important buildings like the University, Parliament and the National Theatre. Norway gained its independence from Sweden in 1905. With the construction of the railway line between Oslo and Bergen (Bergensbanen) in

Christiania from Ekeberg, painting dating from 1840 (Oslo City Museum).

View of the port of Oslo and the City Hall square from Akershus fortress.

1909 and the extension of the port that brought an increase in sea traffic, Christiania became the most important city in the country. In 1925 it reclaimed its old name, Oslo.

During the Second War World (1940 to 1945) Oslo was occupied by German troops. Fortunately the city escaped serious aerial attacks, but an explosion in the port a few days before Christmas 1943 caused considerable damage and loss of life.

Modern Oslo was consolidated with the inauguration of the City Hall in 1950 on the occasion of the city's 900th anniversary (as was then thought).

Today, after the discovery of petrol on Norwegian territory in the 70s, Oslo has become a cosmopolitan city. Commercial and service activities flourish, interesting museums have opened their doors and a large range of cultural activities greets both citizens and visitors. Nor must its international context be forgotten: in particular the award of the Nobel Peace Prize. However, its most important characteristic for our purposes is the opportunity the city offers for enjoying sports and the open-air life. Oslo is undoubtedly a city that is well worth "discovering".

Aker Brygge.

Aerial view of Oslo.

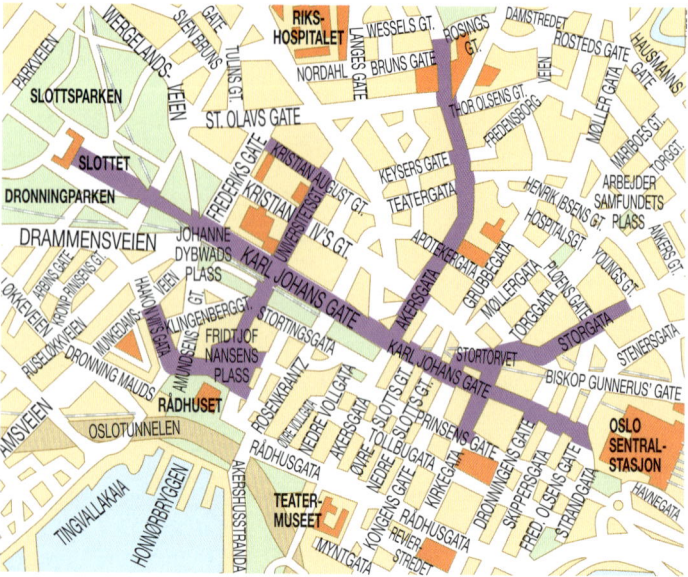

1. KARL JOHANS GATE AVENUE AND SURROUNDINGS

The avenue of Karl Johan is the nerve centre of the capital. It stretches from the Royal Palace at one end to the Central Railway Station in Jernbanetorget Square at the other. Some of the city's and indeed the country's most impressive buildings are sited here.

The **Royal Palace**, where the

17 May 2001: The Norwegian royal family greets their citizens gathered in front of the Royal Palace.

The Royal Palace during the 17 May festival.

Royal Palace: Ball Room.

The sculpture of King Karl Johan and Karl Johan avenue.

Sculpture of Bjørnstjerne Bjørnson, opposite the National Theatre.

National Theatre.

monarch carries out many of his public obligations, is set in the centre of the beautiful **Park of the palace**. Every 17 May, Norway's national day, the royal family greets the procession of children as they file past the palace from one of its balconies. The children in turn greet the king by waving their Norwegian flags. The Royal Palace itself was built during the reign of Carl Johan (in Sweden also known as Carl XIV), whose equestrian statue presides over the palace square. The changing of the guard is held here at 13.30 h.

Going down the avenue towards the railway station we can see the **National Theatre**, home of the Ibsen Festival as well as other theatrical events. Sculptures of Henrik Ibsen (1828-1906) and Bjørnstjerne

University of Oslo.

Bjørnson (1832-1910), the first Norwegian Nobel prize for Literature, majestically preside over the site.

Facing you, on your left, is the oldest building of the **University of Oslo**, founded in 1811. Today with its nearly 40,000 students it is the most important university in the country. It has three buildings, characterised by their yellowish colour and classical appearance. Inside is the Aula Magna (Aulaen), setting of some of the most important events in the history of Oslo and until 1990 where the Nobel Prize for Peace was awarded. The Aula Magna was also for many years the home of the Orchestra of the Philharmonic Company, which achieved international recognition under the baton of its previous conductor, Mariss Janson. The hall is decorated with extraordinary mural freizes by Edvard Munch.

Behind the university, the **National Gallery** founded in 1836, lies Norway's most important fine art museum. A peaceful stroll through its rooms gives its visitors the opportunity to soak up the very soul of Norway by contemplating its landscapes, its peoples and its folklore. Of note are the central rooms, with landscapes by Johan C.C. Dahl, also known as the "the father of Norwegian pictorial art".

National Gallery.

Learning about painting in the National Gallery.

History Museum.

The highlight is one of his best known works, *Vision of the Valley of Fortun,* the famous picture of Tidemand and Gude *The nuptial court in Hardanger,* and *Albertine* by Christian Krogh. Also on show are 58 works of Munch, the father of Expressionism. Outstanding among these are *The Scream, The Frieze of Life, Four Girls on a bridge* and *Self Portrait* (see the section on the Munch Museum in itinerary 5 for further information on Munch).

On the other side of Tullinløkka at Frederiksgate is the **History Museum**, completed in 1902 and one of the most distinguished Modernist buildings in Oslo. It is just one of the University's series of museums on aspects of cultural history. It stages exhibitions ranging in theme from the earliest history of Norway to the Middle Ages. Of particular interest are some objects dating from the time of the Vikings and the room devoted to the Middle Ages, with portals from medieval wooden churches (stavkirker) and sacred art in wood with its original painting. The museum also has an ethnographic section covering non-western cultures, among them the exhibition on Arktis (the arctic regions). It also stages temporary exhibitions on a range of different topics.

The Town Hall seen from the sea shore.

View of the great hall of the City Hall with a mural by Alf Rolfsen.

City Hall: West Gallery.

Returning to Karl Johan Avenue, we now take a detour to the Fridtjof Nansen Square, where the **Oslo City Hall** rises majestically before us. Completed in 1950, it includes a main building with one large and other smaller rooms for holding official celebrations, and two high towers that house the offices of the city administration. The large room and the ceremonial hall have been decorated by Norwegian artists in diverse styles. The motifs used portray the real and legendary history of both city and country from ancient times until the days when

Oslo Concert Hall.

Norway again became a free country, after the Second World War. On the 10th of December every year its central hall becomes the setting for a magnificent ceremony presided over by its king and queen, for the award of the Nobel Peace Prize.

Before returning to Karl Johan Avenue, we can take the opportunity to look over the **Oslo Concert Hall**, one of city's main cultural centres.

Stenersen Museum.

Spikersuppa ("Soup of nails").

Inaugurated in 1977, it was designed by the Finnish architect Åberg and consists of two halls, one with holding 1,700 spectators and the second, 300. It also has one of the biggest organs to be constructed in recent years. Next to the Konserthus, at Munkedamsveien 15, is the **Sternesen Museum**. This museum shows a selection of

View over Eidsvoll Plass with the Grand Hotel and Parliament.

Parliament from Eidsvoll Plass.

Norwegian Art from between 1850 and 1970 including the work of artists such as Ludvig Karsten, Rolf Nesch, Kai Fjell, Jakob Weidemann as well as Edvard Munch.

Back again at Karl Johan Avenue, we next find the gardens of the University, **Studenterlunden**, and **Eidsvoll Square** with the famous Spikersuppa (nail soup). Next to

Interior of Parliament.

The Grand Hotel.

Karl Johan avenue is the most lively street in the city.

this square is **Parliament**, a building constructed between 1861 and 1866 in Romantic Norwegian style. The Norwegian Parliament has two chambers, with 165 seats, many of these held by women, and there is representation of the minority Sami people.

Facing Parliament is the **Grand Hotel**, in whose cafe Henrik Ibsen was for many years a famous and assiduous client. Nowadays, this café and also the **Theaterkaféen** are two of the best options for taking a break or a tasty lunch or dinner.

Before entering the pedestrian area of Karl Johan Avenue, just beyond Parliament we see Akersgaten. Somewhat of a detour along

Church of Saint Olav.

this street allows us to see at close hand various points of interest. On the first section between Karl Johan and Arne Garborg Square, look out for the building of the the present **Ministry of Finance**, dating from the early 20th Century, and that of the **government** **headquarters** (mid-20th Century). In Arne Garborg Square are the **Municipal Library**, founded in 1785, and two churches, **Trefoldighetskirken** and **Margaretakirken**. At the end of Akersgata are the Catholic **Church of Saint Olav,** in a simple Neo Gothic style

View of Telthusbakken and the tower of the Church of Gamle Aker.

Church of Gamle Aker.

with some interesting stained glass windows, and the **Museum of the Applied Arts** exhibiting more than 20,000 pieces of Norwegian craftwork, from the 15th Century to the present.

Stretching out behind the muse-um is the **Vår Frelsers Gravlund Cemetery**, with its area of honour where famous Norwegians are laid to rest. In this area we also find **Telthusbakken**, with its peaceful and beautiful landscapes and its groups of small wooden hous-

Stortorvet (Main Square).

es painted in varying colours, most of which date from the 19th century. And a walk to the highest part of the hill leads you to **Gamle Aker Kirke**, perhaps the oldest stone church in the south of Norway, built around 1080. Near here is Akersveien, a street that also preserves many ancient wooden houses. From here you go back to the church of Saint Olav.

Now it is time to make our way back to Karl Johan, que, between Parliament and the Central Station has become **a pedestrianised street** with shops, large stores, a market, pubs, terraces, cafes, street actors doing their thing, musicians, people wandering about in all directions... This is undoubtedly where you find the best atmosphere in the city during business hours, if weather permits, of course.

In the heart of this area is **Stortorvet**, the old market square with a sculpture of King Christian IV and **Oslo Cathedral**. This cathedral, built in the 17th century and restored in 1950, was where the wedding of Prince Haakon Magnus, heir to the Norwegian throne, was held with Mette-Marit Tjessem Høiby on 25 August 2001. The church is interesting for its late 17th Century altarpiece and pulpit and its stained glass windows, work of Emanuel Vigeland, brother of the famous sculptor.

Oslo City shopping centre.

Around the cathedral is a small covered market selling fruit and antiques, as well as the shops at **Basarhallene**, an unusual market in which you can browse to your heart's content, or simply take the time to enjoy a delicious beer. Next to Stortorvet is Stergata Street and the headquarters of the **Norwegian Opera**.

Interior of the cathedral.

At the end of Karl Johan Avenue, **Jerbanetorget** Square is the setting for the **Central Railway Station**, the bus station **Bussterminalen**, a metro station, tram stops and the stop for trains to and from the airport. From here you can travel to any point in Oslo, the rest of the country or abroad.

Oslo Cathedral.

Basarhallene.

Jerbanetorget Square and the Central Railway Station.

Shopping mall inside the Central Railway Station.

2. AROUND THE PORT: AKERSHUS AND AKER BRYGGE

The port of Oslo is the setting for constant arrivals and departures of the large ferries linking Oslo with Copenhagen, Gøteborg, Kiel and Frederikshaven. Always majestic, always punctual, the large tourist cruisers or the Stena Line, DFDS and Color Line ferries proudly greet the capital.

The area of Oslo with the greatest historic value lies around the **fortress**

View of the port and the Akershus fortress.

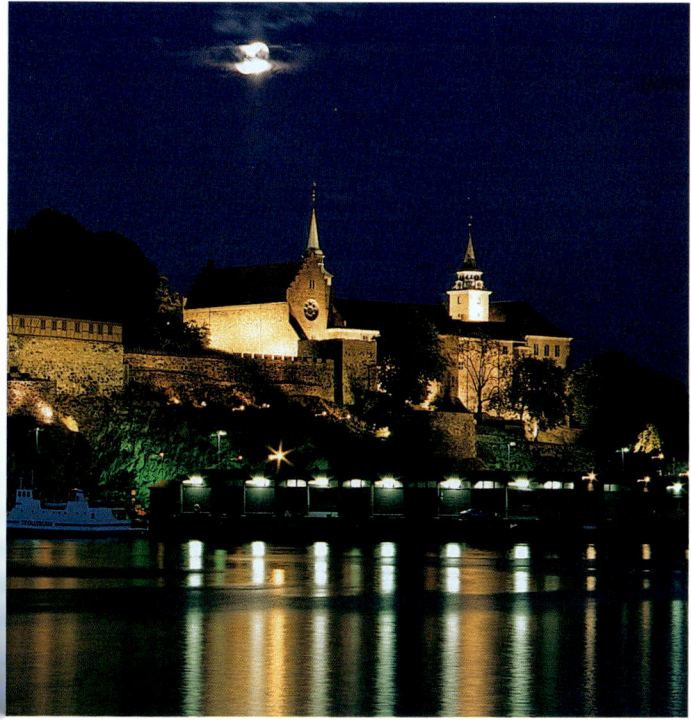

Night-time view of the Akershus fortress.

Gardens and buildings on the site of the fortress.

of **Akershus**, built by King Håkon V at the end of the fjord when he changed the national capital, and which King Christian IV reformed in the Danish Renaissance style in the 17th century. In 1999 the Fortress, celebrated its 700th anniversary: during the course of its history it has been besieged on nine occasions, but never conquered.

At present Akershus is used for large official receptions. It also houses the royal chapel and mausoleum. The best part of this visit are the walks through its gardens, which are a magnificent lookout point over the fjord,

Museum of the Norwegian Resistance.

Museum of Defense.

and a visit to the **Museum of the Norwegian Resistance**, a telling testimony of how the Norwegian people lived through the Second World War. Also here is the **Museum of Defense**, containing a vast assortment of old arms and uniforms. Perhaps the most interesting items amongst its exhibits are its representation of the battle for the heavy water in Telemark, and dioramas depicting the sinking of the cruiser Blücher and the combats at Narvik in 1940.

The best point for viewing the fortress is from Aker Brygge: the tranquil waters of the fjord offer a sparkling, illuminated reflection of the fortress during the long, peaceful nights of the Nordic summer.

Around the fortress itself is **Gamle Christiania**, the oldest district in the city, with its mansions and cobbled streets built by order of Christian IV after of the fire of 1624. One of its most attractive corners is **Christiania Square** which has recovered its former splendour now that the traffic crossing the square has been diverted into underground throughways. Here we can see an original sculpture by Wenche Gulbrandsen known as "The glove of Christian IV" and the former City Hallc building, dating from 1641 and today housing a restaurant and the **Museum of the Theatre**. Through its collection of costumes, curtains, backdrops and posters we can following the history of the Norwegian theatre down through the centuries. Near here, opposite the north wall of the fortress, is a building housing a **model of Christiania in 1838** of interest to anyone wanting to learn more about this city in earlier eras.

The wide range of museums in this area allows visitors a wealth of choice, depending entirely on his or her own particular interests. One of the most interesting is the **Museum of Contemporary Art**, in Bankplassen, a pleasant square. In 1857 one of the oldest surviving restaurants in Oslo - the **Café Engebret** - opened there in its 18th Century building. The Museum of Contemporary Art occupies the

Christiania Square: the sculpture "The glove of Christian IV".

Museum of Contemporary Art.

former headquarters of the Bank of Norway, an Art Nouveau style building dating from the early 20th century.

Almost next door, at Kongensgate 4, is the **Museum of Norwegian Architecture**, devoted to Norwegian

Engebret Café.

architecture over the last thousand years. This also occupies an old, now restored palace whose patio has been covered with a glass dome. The **Astrup Fearnley Museum of Modern Art** at Dronningensgate 4 has a permanent collection of works by the main post-war Norwegian artists and also organises temporary exhibitions.

Norwegian Museum of Architecture.

Astrup Fearnley Museum.

Lying between the fortress and Aker Brygge is the **Rådhusplassen or Square of the City Hall**, where the maritime façade of the City Hall and the silhouette of Saint Hall-vard, patron saint of the city, are

The port and Aker Brygge from Akershus fortress.

notable features. At one end is the old Railway station serving the west (Vestbanestasjonen), which has been declared an artistic heritage site. There are currently several projects afoot for the area, one of which involves the building of a Peace Museum (Fredsmuseum). Ferries leaving for the peninsula of Bygdøy and ships making tourist excursions on the fjord leave from the dock of this square.

The streets around **Aker dock (Aker Brygge)** offer the best and most exciting street entertainment. The site used to house the most important shipyards and dockside warehouses in Norway. After rehabilita-

tion these now provide a shopping and entertainment centre with a wide choice of leisure options: shops with all the best brands, restaurants for all budgets, kiosks, terraces, musicians, cinemas, exhibitions, an IMAX cinema, historical and modern architecture - in short, the most fantastic ambience in the city. This is particularly so at dusk, when Norwegians sit down to chat around a beer and a dish of prawns or one of the many terraces, while dusk descends, the ferries cross and re-cross the fjord, seagulls cry and the salty smell of the sea tickles your nose. This is the magic of summer nights in Oslo.

Aker Brygge and the City Hall.

3. BYGDØY AND ITS MUSEUMS

The peninsula of Bygdøy, some 5 km from the city centre, is the most sought-after residential area in the city. Home of politicians, artists and ambassadors, it offers an idyllic environment of woods and beaches only a few minutes out of the city centre. Bygdøy is also the setting of some of the most interesting museums in Oslo and so has a great appeal for tourists. The best way to get there is by the ferry that leaves from the City Hall square and gets you to the peninsula in around 15 minutes. Or take the number 30 bus to Bygdøy from the centre (National Theatre).

Several of these museums deal with the history of the Norwegians and the sea: the Museum of the Viking Ships, the Fram Museum, the Kon-Tiki Museum and the Norwegian Marine Museum. All together offer the most fascinating testimony of the many and dramatic vicissitudes of the Norwegians over fjords, seas and oceans. The other large museum in Bygdøy is the Norwegian Folk Museum.

If you are travelling to Bygdøy by bus, you will travel along the fjord. Along the way can be seen a series of boats of all sizes in which the Norwegians sail the waters of the fjord during the peaceful summer days. This picture reminds us that in this country, with its long maritime tradition, there is an average of one boat for every four inhabitants. At times, in the centre of the bay, you can see the royal yacht anchored. Entering Bygdøy by land you also pass the **Royal Residence of Bygdøy**, where the royal family resides during the summer months.

Just before arriving at the Folk Museum, a small road on the left leads to **Oscarshall**, a Tudor-style palace built in the mid-19th Century by the king who presided over the union with Sweden, Oscar I. At present, this shows a collection of 19th Century drawings from the Norwegian Romantic period.

Now we reach the **Norwegian Folk Museum**, a mosaic of the rich Norwegian culture. Invest half a day in this marvellous tour of Nor-

View of Oslo fjord from the Huk beach on the Bygdøy Peninsula.

The Oscarshall Palace.

A view of the Norwegian Folk Museum.

vegian traditions, you won't regret it! Created in 1894, this is one of the oldest museums of its kind in the world. Divided into different sections, the star of which is its open-air museum. This consists of 170 meticulously restored wooden buildings taken from locations throughout Norway: painted farmhouses from Telemark, cabins from Gudbrandsdal, farms from the Setesdal valleys, Oppland, Numedal, etc., and a Sami camp. Polite young people dressed in the traditional costumes of the different regions show you over the farmhouses and the old way of life. The jewel of the museum is its wooden church, the Stavkyrken, from Gol. Built around 1170 and transferred to the museum in 1885, the church is very well preserved. On the side oppo-

Girls dressed in traditional costume in the Norwegian Folk Museum.

Building of the Viking Ship Museum.

site the museum, after crossing the central square next to its entrance, we reach the Christiania district with its buildings dating back to old Oslo.

The museum's large central building houses permanent and temporary exhibitions. Outstanding are the magnificent collection of Norwegian folk costumes and the exhibition devoted to the culture of the Samis of Lapland. The museum rounds off its activities with folk music groups and other open air activities.

A few metres down the road is the **Viking Ship Museum**, which is another of the University's museums of cultural history. This museum displays the best-preserved Viking ships in the world, discovered in three large tumuli near Oslo fjord. They were buried here so that their royal owners could use them on their last journey to the world of the dead. Also on show

are unique pieces of Viking art and simple objects that bear witness to the day-to-day life of the Vikings. The archaeological heritage of the Norwegian Vikings is divided between the University museums. Arms, crafts and jewels are housed in the Museum of History in the city centre and the Viking Ship Museum exhibits the ships and funerary items. The objects of greatest interest for visitors will certainly be those exhibited in the Viking Ship Museum, a dedicated to the tumuli where the ships were found, and built between 1926 and 1932 by the well-known Norwegian architect Arnstein Arneberg, also one of the architects responsible for the City Hall project.

The building is divided into five sections. In the first is the Oseberg, the best-preserved and many think the most impressive Viking ship of all. It was built around 800 and found in 1904. It seems it was the tomb of a Viking queen, Åse, who was buried with a servant and many of her belongings.

To the left we find the Gokstad ship, dug up in 1880 and a *balandra* (boat of war), very hydrodynamic, strong and safe; it was in this type of ship that the Vikings embarked on their adventures across the high oceans. A copy of the Gokstad ship was sent to Chicago on the occasion of the 1893 world exhibition, where it is still displayed today in one of the city's museums.

In the bay on the right are the remains of the ship Tune. Found in 1867, but impossible to restore, it nevertheless gives us an insight into the solid construction, safety and the ingeniousness which the Vikings put into their ships.

At the end of the building, an exhibition shows the objects found in the boats: cloth, shoes, kettles, arms, harnesses, cooking utensils, in short, an open book on the Viking "modus vivendi". A trolley, three sleighs and some magnificent masts all confirm that the Viking culture reached sur-

The Oseberg ship.

prising and at times sophisticated heights of development.

You must not miss the small but important, exhibition on the first floor about the westward voyages and expeditions made by the Vikings to Vinland. It includes an interesting model of a Viking village and a showcase with reproductions of objects found in the remains of the settlements in L'Anse-Aux-Meadows, on the north coast of Newfoundland. These are simple objects - a

The Gokstad ship.

GOKSTADSKIBET.

The Tune ship.

brooch, a lamp and ballast material - but provide incontestable evidence of the arrival of the Vikings in America some 500 years before Columbus.

Continuing along the road some 10 minutes on foot or in the little train, always between magnificent mansions, you arrive at a small square, round which are sited three most unusual museums: the Norwegian Marine Museum, the Fram Museum and the Kon-Tiki Museum.

The **Norwegian Marine Museum** has a surprising collection of models that tracks the entire history of the Norwegians and the sea, from the most primitive fishing boats to large whalers. The museum also has a cinema with an 180 degree screen where they project a spectacular film by Ivo Caprino that shows the Norwegian coast in times of storm and calm, under the heat of the summer and the cold of the winter. There is also a restaurant and outside a kiosk serving coffee and light food and a terrace with

Aerial view of the Norwegian Marine Museum, the Fram and the Kon-Tiki ships.

Norwegian Marine Museum

a fantastic view over the fjord and the city of Oslo.

The **Fram Museum** is a surprise too, partly because of its architecture. It contains the polar ship Fram, built in 1892 in Larvik by Colin Archer for the first expedition to the North Pole by Fridtjof Nansen (1861-1930). Nansen, who had already crossed the ices of Greenland on skis at the age of 27, decided to get as near as possible to the North Pole by following the polar currents. To do this he needed a ship of the size of the Fram that could stand the pressures of the polar ices. Nansen carried out the expedition between 1893 and 1896, and reached the latitude 86 degrees 14 minutes North. The expedition was a success and converted Nansen into a national hero. Years later, in 1911, Roald Amundsen (1872-1928) was the first to reach the South Pole, on board the Fram.

The Fram's subsequent fate was uncertain until the second Norwegian polar explorer, Otto Sverdrup, managed to rescue it in time and had a museum built for its preservation.

The ship is kept just as it was, and you can walk all the way down it from the bridge to the keel. Our visit to the museum ends with maps and spectacular photographs that give us some idea of the harshness and drama of the adventures of the great Norwegian explorers.

The **Kon-Tiki Museum** is the last piece in this display of the intense coexistence of the Norwegians and the sea. The museum tells the story of the voyages by the anthropologist Thor Heyerdahl

Fram Museum, the Fram ship and detail of the ship.

(1914-2002). Heyerdahl wanted to demonstrate through his voyages the connections between the great primitive cultures. In 1947, on board the Kon-Tiki raft, built from wood following techniques used by the original inhabitants of South America, set off on a voyage with a crew of four Norwegians and a Swede. The journey lasted 101 days. Following the Humboldt current,

Entrance to the Kon-Tiki Museum.

from Callao (Peru) to Raroia Island in French Polynesia. The original raft is laid out so that it can also be seen from below.

In 1969, at the foot of the pyramid of Giza, Heyerdahl built the ship RA, using papyrus, just as the Egyptians had done ancient times. 14 metres long and also with a multi-ethnic crew, it set sail from Safi (Morocco) for Barbados.

The raft sank before arriving at its destination. Heyerdahl then built a second raft, RA II, which is exhibited in the museum, and managed to make the crossing in eight weeks. This happened a year later, in 1970.

The museum offers an overview of all Heyerdahl's expeditions: Fatu Hiva, the Galapagos, Easter Island, etc. From his Tigris expedition along the Persian Gulf only part of the burnt rudder remains.

Heyerdahl decided to burn this in Djibouti as a protest against the many wars being fought in the area.

A beautiful symbol of peace in a world of wars. Films of Thor Heyerdahl's voyages are projected in a small cinema on site. Try not to miss the documentary "Kon-Tiki" (English version). This film will make it easy to understand the genius of this project and of the man who carried it out.

Return to Oslo. You can take the ship that leaves the dock next to the Fram Museum back to the Town Hall square.

Before reach we will pass by the **schooner Gjøa**, with the that Roald Amundsen cross for the first time the straight of Bering and became the conquered of Nordvestpassasjen (the route sea at the north of the continent American).

The RA II and the Kon-Tiki rafts.

4. FROM THE NATIONAL THEATRE TO VIGELAND PARK

From the National Theatre we set off towards the west of the city to visit various points of interest, ending up in Vigeland Park. We first skirt round the **gardens of the Royal Palace**, always open to the public. The statue of Queen Maud, wife of Haakon VII, greets us from its pedestal nestling among the trees.

Gardens of the Royal Palace: the Royal Guard.

Sculpture of Queen Maud in the gardens of the Royal Palace.

Office of Henrik Ibsen (Ibsen Museum).

Portrait of Henrik Ibsen, work of Gustav J. Gulickson (Ibsen Museum).

Kofi Annan, Nobel Prize for Peace 2001, greets the citizens of Oslo from a balcony of the Grand Hotel.

Next we go to the **Ibsen Museum**, that offers a stroll through the life and work of that most universal of Norwegian writers, Henrik Ibsen (1828-1906), with a visit to the writer's personal office. A must for lovers of literature.

Immediately past the Royal Palace gardens on our right is the **Nobel Institute**, a yellowish Neo Classical building presided over by the bust of the brilliant Swedish inventor.

This is here where every year the five members of the Nobel Committee deliberate and cast their votes to choose the Nobel Peace Prize. The prize is awarded each year in the City Hall on 10 December, the anniversary of the death of Alfred Nobel (1833-1896), always coinciding with the award of the other Nobel Prizes in Stockholm. No-one knows for sure why Nobel, when drawing up his will, conceded this honour to the Norwegian Parliament. It may be that since Norway and Sweden formed a union at the time, it seemed natural that one of the prizes should be awarded by Norway.

After the **National Library** we arrive at one of the most elegant streets in the city, **Bygdøy allé**, quite a spectacle in spring when the chestnut trees are in flower.

Go on upwards and turn right along Thomas Heftyes street, which takes you through one of the most elegant and expensive residential districts of Oslo, to **Frogner Park**.

Vigeland Park: the bridge with the bronze sculptures and the Monolith.

With its 32 hectares, Frogner Park is the biggest park in the city, a green lung right at its centre. Both in summer and winter this is the favourite place of Oslo inhabitants for a stroll, to go jogging, play tennis, or do nothing at all and simply relax and enjoy the sun if it happens to be out.

Inside the park you can admire the sculptures of Gustav Vigeland, a heartfelt tribute to mankind. Given that this has become the most-visited tourist attraction in the country, the park is best-known as Vigeland Park. Surely it is time for UNESCO to decide to include this wonderful work on their lists of "Heritage Sites of Mankind?

Gustav Vigeland (1869-1943) trained as a sculptor under the influence of the classical world and the Danish artist, Bertel Torvaldsen. In 1921, and in exchange for a small workshop-dwelling, he offered all his work to the city of Oslo, which put them at his disposal in the area that has since become Vigeland Park.

From 1924 on and during a period of almost twenty years, Vige-

Sculpture beside the Monolith.

"The angry boy".

"The Fountain and Tree of Life".

land worked in the park. He created 212 sculptures in bronze, iron and granite, with a total of 671 figures. The artist managed to complete all the work he started, but did not live to see its definitive exhibition. Nor did he ever explain whether he had decided to give his sculptures any special meaning. All we can say is that they allow an infinite number of interpretations, and form a spectacular reflection on the human condition: its great moments, its emotions and its conflicts, are here majestically expressed for the inspiration of future generations.

You enter the park through a set of spectacular wrought iron gates, also designed by Vigeland. The park takes us on a slow journey round the cycle of life, from birth (in the small circular space on the edge of the lake, dropped down a level), through youth and on to maturity (the 58 sculptures lining both sides of the bridge). In a second phase, Vigeland develops the subject of the "Fountain and the Tree of Life": a colossal fountain held up by three Atlases pours out water for life, nature and man. From the "Tree of Life" hang babies, young people, fathers and mothers, children, old people and death. The cycle is repeated on the friezes below.

On the way up the stairs leading to the Monolith there are 36 granite sculptures that reflect the different ages in the cycle of life. In the Monolith itself, 17 metres high, 121 figures intertwine dramatically, striving to reach a summit that is finally conquered by a child. This part of the park ends with an astral clock marking the horoscope, symbolising the passage of time, and a wheel with 7 bodies intertwined, where life and death, the beginning and the end, complete the cycle.

All these large-scale sculptures are outstanding for their expressive and dramatic qualities. But for various reasons some of these have become particularly popular: the newborn child by the lakeside, the angry boy in the bridge (which has now been

Vigeland Museum: building with a room in the artist's studio.

adopted as the symbol of the city of Oslo), the Atlantes bearing on their shoulders the heavy weight of the fountain of life, the children playing happily among the branches of the tree of life, the two angry children and the old people in the upper to the monolith.

And, above all, that column depicting struggling life, that monolith of hope wrested by the artist from a single block of granite, that double triumph, artistic and human, of man that year on year goes on disturbing or at least questioning the soul of everyone who visits this extraordinary testimony to human life that that - the work itself and the park that surrounds it - forms a master work indeed.

Anyone interested in the work of Vigeland can visit his workshop, near the cafe, now converted into the **Vigeland Museum**. Here can be seen drawings, maquette, projects, models of the sculptures and the history of the park and its creation.

The park is open 24 hours a day, and entrance is always free. So if you can, pay another visit at dusk or at night when it is lit up and incidentally, quite safe. It is even more moving and impressive when seen in the golden rays of dusk or by the silvery light of the long Scandinavian summer night, with its lights and its shadows, bathed in peace and silence.

Vigeland Park is also home to another museum, the **Oslo City**

Oslo City Museum.

4. From the National Theatre to Vigeland Park

The crossroads of Dronningensgate and Tollbugata streets in the 19th century, watercolour by Anna Diriks (Oslo City Museum).

Museum, housed in a late-17th Century building near the main entrance of the park on the left. With the design of a residential villa of its era, it preserves valuable original furniture and displays models, engravings and paintings illustrating the development of the city over the centuries.

Room in the Oslo City Museum.

5. THE MUNCH MUSEUM AND THE BOTANICAL GARDEN

The **Munch Museum** is to the east of the city. It is easy to get to: You can take bus number 20 from Majorstua or else take the metro and get off at the Tøyen stop (all lines going east).

Edvard Munch is one of the greatest painters in the Nordic countries, and his work reflects some of the key issues of the art of the end of the 19th and start of the 20th Centuries: the anguish of life, solitude, fear and death.

This subject matter and his characteristic style of work together made Munch the father of pictorial Expressionism. It demonstrates its force to us in its strong, violent and at times clashing colours and lines.

Munch was born in Løten in 1863, but as a child moved to Christiania.

Child of a very religious military doctor and a young mother, 20 years younger than his father, he grew up surrounded by illness and death. His mother died of tuberculosis when he was 5 years old.

His older sister also died of the same illness. Another brother died just after he got married. His younger sister suffered from a mental illness, and the artist himself was ill for much of his childhood.

He studied painting and drawing with the great master Christian Krogh. He therefore began as a

5. The Munch Museum and the Botanical Garden

Realist, and was an active participant in the artistic bohemia of Christiania. He travelled successively to Paris and Berlin where he extended his artistic training, taking him into the Expressionist movement. But Munch returns constantly in his work to the recollection of illness, death and hardship, themes that are present in all his work This explains why rather than pleasing us, Munch's pictures make us uneasy.

Munch's paintings alternate between portraying the countryside - sometimes natural, sometimes symbolic - of his native Norway, and dramatic interior scenes of melancholy, illness and death under the tenuous Nordic light. Thus the small coastal village of Åsgårdstrand, near Horten, become the real and metaphorical setting for many of the author's landscape compositions. His family and his friends become the other great protagonists in his work, interrogating us about the sense of life, from the *The Girls on the bridge* to The Sick Child or the now mythical The Scream, of which he painted several versions.

Munch finished what is perhaps his best known work *The Scream*

Munch Museum

Self Portrait of the artist, in the Munch Museum.

in 1893. It is considered one of the first great works of Expressionism, the most definitive example of work that emerges from within the artist, from his very soul. Its extreme colours, emphatic lines, the almost grotesque distortion of the face all express an anguish that emerges from the artist's subconscious or soul. The painting finally reaches out beyond the conflicts of the artist himself to bring a sense of "fin-du-siècle", anguish and apocalypse to

"Stemmen 1893" (The Voice) in the Munch Museum.

5. The Munch Museum and the Botanical Garden

A view of the Botanical Garden and Museum.

Greenhouse in the Botanical Garden.

all who view it. This is its universal appeal.

Before his death in 1944, Munch left the whole of his work to the town of Oslo.

The Munch Museum opened in 1963. It has more than 1,100 paintings, 4,700 drawings and 15,500 lithographs, on more than 700 topics, and the work is exhibited on a rotating basis. A stroll through its modern rooms guarantees you a special insight into the artist's soul. Thus Oslo offers us not only the collection in the National Gallery but also the most comprehensive vision of this artistic genius. This makes the city a must on the itinerary of every real art lover.

Near the Munch Museum is the **botanical garden**. This is a beautiful site with remarkable flowers, shrubs and trees, a special garden made up of stones, greenhouses with tropical plants and four different museums: the **Botanical Museum** devoted particularly to Norwegian flora; the **Geological and Mineralogy Museum** which as well as showing an extensive collection of minerals also relates the history of the geological formation of the country; the **Palaeontology Museum** with its great variety of fossil plants and animals and reproductions of paintings and prehistoric inscriptions; and the **Zoological Museum** which gives special attention to Norwegian fauna.

Zoological Museum.
Geological Museum.

Sculpture of King Olav going cross country skiing and the Holmenkollen ski-jump.

AROUND OSLO

The surroundings of Oslo let you have your first close contact with nature in Norway and will surprise you in more ways than one: a splendid natural environment, spectacular landscapes, interesting buildings and very attractive museums. A veritable symphony of nature and culture.

Holmenkollen

The **Holmenkollen ski jump** is 417 metres above sea level. It was built in 1892 and has been reformed on seven different occasions. It can be reached from the city centre by metro, although the best way to get there is by car, making a steady panoramic ascent through one of the most beautiful residential areas not only in Oslo but in the whole of Scandinavia. You can take the car to the foot of the ski jump, and view the city from its gallery. Inside the ski-jump is a lift that goes up to a height of 60 metres above the ground. From the top of the ski jump, the view above Oslo and its fjord is extraordinary. You can also get some idea of the organisation of Scandinavian cities, always surrounded by and immersed in a natural setting. And don't let us forget that Oslo means "the wood of the gods".

Next door is the **Skiing Museum**, which exhibits one of the oldest skis in Norway, found in Alvdal and more than 1,400 years old, as well as equipment, materials and clothing from the expeditions

The Holmenkollen ski-jump in summer and winter.

The Holmenkollen ski-jump.

of Nansen and Amundsen. Holmenkollen is very popular with the inhabitants of Oslo, and ideal for making excursions. In summer they go path-walking and in winter skiing. Can you imagine it, leaving work, taking the metro, buckling on your skis and making you way back down to the city? Few cities can offer anything like it.

Skiing Museum.

Oslo fjord and the Holmenkollen ski-jump.

Ever since 1892 they have been organising competitions at the Holmenkollen ski-jump. On Holmenkollen day, in March, thousands of Norwegians, many on foot, come to join one of the most popular skiing events of the winter.

Do not miss a visit to the **Holmenkollen Park Hotel Rica,** located at the end of the ski-jump to the right. This beautiful building was built around the end of last century in the so-called "dragon style" (style of Norwegian construction based on knowledge of the architectural trends of Viking times), with red-painted walls, sloping roofs and ornamentation in the form of dragons' heads. One of the few and priceless examples that still remain in the whole of the country.

Celebration of the Day Holmenkollen.

Tryvann

Only a few kilometres up-mountain from Holmenkollen is the **Tryvann communications tower (Tryvannstårnet)**, 118.5 m high.

Skiing around Tryvan.

A lift inside carries you up 60 metres, taking you to 588 metres above sea level; on very clear days you can see more than 30,000 km2 and sometimes even as far as Sweden. Up here, the air is always pure and fresh. In this sea of green woods there are a host of tracks and pathways to ski down in winter, or stroll or take a refreshing swim in one of its many lakes in summer. Did you know that within the Oslo city boundaries there is a grand total of 343 lakes?

If you walk further on you reach a lookout point with a sculpture portraying Mr Krag, director-general of roads, who was responsible for the construction of the road itself. From here there is a fantastic panoramic view over the city, the fjord, the woods and the distant snow-covered mountains. In the distance is the 1,883 m high Peak of Gausta.

A stroll by the Oslo fjord

The **Oslo fjord**, that flows into the Skagerak, is some 104 km long, just half as long as Sognefjord, the longest of the Norwegian fjords.

The Tryvann tower in winter and summer.

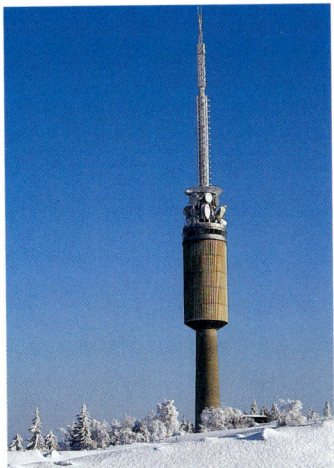

Oslo and the fjord from Hovedøya Island.

It has two main channels, but only communicates with the open sea to the west. Solid ground, islands, islets, coves, beaches, woods, fields and marine fauna have over the centuries combined to form an idyllic environment, food and riches for the whole community that lives on its banks, right up to the capital.

From the City Hall dock, various companies offer a tour up Oslo fjord. Crossings can take anything from one hour to a whole day. But even one hour might be enough to capture the essence of this magnificent excursion. We recommend you to go at dusk. After a day spent walking all over the city, there is no more delightful and relaxing feeling than letting yourself drift away on a boat. Float by islets, beautiful country houses, boats and yachts, beaches and coves. Enjoy the penetrating smell of the sea and the scream of the seagulls, a symphony of light and colour in a splendid natural context. An unforgettable experience, the best aperitif you could have before discovering the extraordinary fjords on the west coast. If you prefer, you can even find a boat where you can take a light snack or a full lunch or dinner. This is the time to sample some delicious prawns with bread, butter and beer, or some tasty smoked meats: salmon, trout and the always excellent herring.

In **Hovedøya**, the island nearest the city, are the ruins of a monastery founded by Cistercian monks in the 12th century, four centuries later being sacked and burnt and never reconstructed.

In a corner of the fjord towards the south-east of Bygdøy on the Høvikodden peninsula (12 km to the south-east of the centre) is the **Henie Onstad Art Centre** open in 1969 by the famous skater, Olympic champion, and then popular actress Sonja Henie and her husband, the ship owner Niels Onstad. Its main object is to display international contemporary art in all its aspects (the figurative arts, theatre, cinema, music, dance, etc.). The centre's collections of Cubism, Surrealism and Abstract Art are particularly interesting.

Tusenfryd and Vikinglandet

This visit is very much to be recommended, above all if you have children with you. **Tusenfryd** is a conventional Amusement Park located to the south of the city. **Vikinglandet** is a theme park next to the Amusement Park on the life of the Vikings, with reproductions of dragons and actors disguised as Vikings, among other ideas. Vikinglandet plunges you into the past and spirits you back in time to the Viking world, in the

Hovedøya (Large Island).

country where these Norsemen did their most heroic deeds. The 541 bus from the central bus station takes some 20 minutes to get you to both parks along the E-6 road.

Kongens utsit (The view of the king)

Near Oslo, along the E-18 towards Hønefoss, is **"Kongens utsikt"**, one of the most impressive panoramic viewing points in the south of Norway, surrounded by great woods where kings used to go hunting in days of old. To get there, leave Oslo by the E-18.

All along the fjord you will see some of the city's many sailing clubs. At the turnoffs to Bygdøy and Fornebu (Oslo's former airport) you reach the Henie-Onstad Art Centre.

Go straight on, turn right at Sandvika and continue up to Sollihøgda. The view over the fjord of Tyri is breathtaking.

At Sundøya, turn left towards Dronningveien (Path of the Queen), a private toll road. Follow this road to the end, stop at Kleivstua and take a 20-minute stroll into the wood. If you do not want to or cannot walk through the woody land, you will

Nordmarka: the countryside around Oslo offers interesting landscapes.

The Skibladner boat on Lake Mjøsa.

be sufficiently rewarded by just stopping to marvel at the view from the highest part of Dronningveien.

Akershus and Oppland

These are Oslo's two neighbouring provinces.

Their surroundings are really an open invitation to submerge yourself in nature: Oslo fjord, the woods and lakes that surround the city allow you to tune in to nature: fishing, rambling, skiing and hunting (in season), bathing, sailing... Any corner, with its tranquillity and exuberant greenery, offers a good pretext to get away from the city, even if only for a day.

You can get there by ferry, car or train. Below we suggest some alternatives:

Catch the train to **Gjøvik,** a beautiful city on Lake Mjøsa, the biggest lake in Norway. You can also go by train or car (170 km north of Oslo by the E6) to **Lillehammer**, site of the 1994 Winter Olympic Games.

Stroll along Storgata (Main Street), visit the Olympic stadium, the open-air museum at **Maihaugen**, or take a turn around Lake Mjøsa in the **Skibladner**, one of the few extant operational paddle boats. Take in the beautiful and peaceful landscapes, replete with the farmhouses, villages, fields and woods so representative of the inland regions of Norway. On board they serve "Skibladner", a traditional dish: fresh salmon steamed with new potatoes and Sandefjord butter, and for dessert, strawberries and cream.

Gardermoen Airport.

USEFUL RECOMMENDATIONS

Getting to Oslo

The capital of Norway is very easy to get to. By car, the best access is by the E-6 road from Sweden via Gøteborg, or by the E-18 from Stockholm.

The train will take you from Stockholm or Copenhagen right to the city centre.

Access by sea is also frequent: DFDS has a daily ferry service between Copenhagen and Oslo, a magnificent voyage of 16 hours stopping off in Helsinborg (Sweden). Color Line also operates daily services from Kiel (Germany) to Oslo, a voyage of around 20 hours.

Both boats leave you in the heart of the city. Oslo also has a daily ferry connection with the ports of Hirtshals and Frederikshavn in the north of Jutland. Although undoubtedly the fastest way to travel is by air: SAS and Braathen offer direct flights or flights via Copenhagen, and domestic flights that connect with any point in the country.

Oslo **Gardemoen** airport is 50 km north of the capital by the E-6 road. From there it is easy to get to the city centre. By car this takes around 45 minutes. A taxi

trip would be quite expensive. The airport bus, the Flybussen, takes you to the centre in 45 minutes. The quickest way to reach Oslo is by fast train (Flutoget) connecting the capital with the airport every 15 minutes, taking 19 minutes in all.

Prices

In Oslo and throughout the country in general, the standard of living is high, and this is reflected in the cost of living. Here are some prices for your guidance. A return tram or metro ticket, the best way to get around the city, costs 20 crowns, but it gives you

60 minutes to make as many changes of line as you wish. Making a phone call from a public phonebox is relatively cheap, whether using a telephone card (on sale in any newsagent's) or with coins, and it is cheaper to call at night. To call abroad, dial: 00 + the country code + the phone number.

Alcohol and tobacco are heavily taxed. Alcoholic drinks with an alcohol content of more than 4.75 degrees can only be bought at outlets of Vinmonopolet (the state alcohol monopoly). The water is good everywhere, and can be drunk straight from the tap. To

Sculpture beside the Oslo Concert Hall. In the background, Victoria Terrasse.

accompany their food the Scandinavians usually drink water, mineral water, beer or wine. In the case of dishes with a high fat content or on traditional festivals, for example for breakfast on the 17th of May, they consume akevitt (Norwegian eau-de-vie). Try it, you'll have no regrets – it is strong but delicious.

Tips

In Scandinavia it is customary to give a tip, approximately 10%, when service is good.

Weather

Given that Oslo is at a latitude of 60°, the capital does not have an excessively cold climate: temperatures are pleasant in spring and autumn and in summer it is definitely "hot", but winter is certainly cold! In Oslo, in winter, the snow can sometimes last for 4 to 6 months, from December to April, and conditions for skiing are superb. In autumn and particularly in winter the days are short, but in spring and above all in summer, they are very long indeed. At the height of summer, the city can enjoy some 20 hours of light.

In spite of its pleasant climate in spring and summer, you should not trust the weather. If anything characterises Scandinavian weather it is its extreme and rapid changes. They say that the first subject of conversation between the Norwegians is the weather, and rain can be so frequent, so endless, that the Norwegians prefer to say "it's not raining, it's just the tears of Odin".

Always have an umbrella and a raincoat to hand. And just in case, a jersey or cover-up to cope with a brusque change of temperatures.

Shopping

Oslo offers an interesting commercial life, with varied opening hours.

The best shops are to be found along Karl Johan Avenue and many normally have special offers in the summer months.

Other important shopping centres are Glasmagasinet (in Stortorvet), Oslo City, Sentralstasjonen (Central Railway Station) and Aker Brygge.

The opening hours of the large shopping centres are usually from 10.00 h. to 20.00 h. on weekdays and from 10.00 h. to 16.00 h. on Saturdays.

You can buy a large variety of souvenirs, both in Oslo and in the rest of the country, particularly at the main points of tourist interest. Prices tend to be the same all over the country. It is not the custom to haggle, and payment is made in Norwegian crowns or any other legal currency.

Highlights among the great variety of items on sale are jerseys in Norwegian wool (the most prestigious being the "Dale of Norway" make), reproductions of Viking craftwork (figurines, boats, ashtrays, jewels) Lapland crafts (knives, pendants, letter openers made from reindeer horn, jewels), trolls in all shapes and sizes, beautifully illustrated books about

Typical Norwegian knitted jerseys.

Norway, the music of Grieg, tee-shirts, etc. If you want to buy salmon, seafood or pre-cooked food, you should go to specialist shops.

Some items that you can only find in Oslo are tee-shirts and books on the city, particularly the City Hall and Vigeland Park, and good lithographs and reproductions of the most famous works of Munch.

Two of the most specialist souvenir shops in Oslo are the shop of the Museum of Viking boats, with reproductions of exclusive jewellery from the era of the Vikings, and the shop Juhls, with crafts and jewellery from Lapland, in Roald Amundsen street near the City Hall.

Finally, do not forget to ask for Tax Free prices and the relevant

Viking craftwork.

receipts for your payments. In the shop you will pay the price marked on the article, but before you leave the country, by duly presenting these receipts, you will be returned 10 or 15% or even more of the amount paid.

Food and restaurants
In general, the quality of restaurants in Oslo is good and prices are reasonable.
Breakfast, served from 7 to 10

Troll.

in the morning, is abundant. In hotels it is almost invariably a buffet: juices, cheeses, eggs, sausages, yoghurts, cereals, toast and herring (marinated, in tomato, curried... and always excellent); with bread, butter, tea or coffee as base.

Lunch, between 12.00 h. and 14.00 h., is lighter; it normally consists of delicious canapés covered with a large selection of cold meats.

Dinner is usually more substantial. It is usual to serve a starter of soup or other aperitifs, and then a second course of prime quality meat or fish followed by dessert and coffee.

Another very typical type of meal throughout Scandinavia both for lunch and dinner is the free Buffet or "koldtbordet" (cold table). This is a buffet with a great assortment of starters (salads, sausages, smoked meats, prawns), two or three dishes of meat and fish to choose from, and various cheeses and desserts.

You can go back as often as you like, but it is better to follow a definite order like that specified above and ration your portions if you do not want to fill up quickly. On your trip to Norway you should give it a try. It is served in some restaurant and many hotels.

Smoked salmon.

Assortment of prawns.

Among the many good restaurants in Oslo we can recommend the Theatercafeen and that of the Grand Café.

These are classical establishments offering good quality and good service. In the Aker Brygge area there are restaurants for all tastes and budgets: for a light lunch or dinner Herbern offers great prawns, and the chain Peppes Pizzas – found all over the city – offers excellent pizzas, pies and salads; in Louise restaurant good French and international food is served, good quality and good service; and the Lofoten restaurant serves very good fish, but the prices are very high indeed.

For those who prefer something simpler and more economical we recommend the Kaffistova cafe at the Hotel Bondeheimen. Here you can find self-service fare at reasonable prices – canapés and typical Norwegian dishes like kjøttkaker (meat balls), rømmegrøt (sour cream porridge) and pytt-i-panne (an egg dish with meat and potato leftovers). Do not miss the "softis" (icecream) covered in chocolate sauce. This is also on sale in kiosks all along Aker Brygge.

Lamb stew and cabbage.

Theatre, opera, concerts and other entertainment

Oslo has a busy cultural life: music, concerts, opera, theatre... The National Theatre and the many theatres to be found all over the city offer everything from Ibsen classics to opera and the great musicals that triumph in London and New York. The season begins in late August, when the **Ibsen Festival** starts in the National Theatre, going on the end of June. July and August, when the city is alive with tourists, are holiday months and so theatrical activity is almost non-existent.

However, in summer you can attend shows of popular dance, always interesting and entertaining in a country where folk tales, popular music and regional costumes form an important part of the national spirit, and demonstrate the cultural variety and prosperity of the country's different regions. **Leikarringen BUL (BUL popular dance group)** has a show at 20.30 h. every Thursday in July and August in the Oslo Konserthus.

In Aker Brygge, at night and when weather permits, there is an incredible bustle. Here people can stroll, chat, have a drink and listen to live music.

The most important festival popular of the year in Norway is 17 May, **the National Festival of Norway**, which in Oslo has its own special traditions.

On this important day for the Norwegians, family and friends meet up to have breakfast together and then a children's procession begins.

Tens of thousands of children, dressed in their best clothes and each with a Norwegian flag, walk in procession down Karl Johan avenue to the Royal Palace, where the royal family greets them from the balcony.

Another very popular festival is

Performances by Norwegian Opera.

the **Holmenhollen Day**, that in March brings together thousands of Norwegians in Holmenkollen. But there are also events like the **Festivals of jazz**, the **Festival of chamber music** or the **children's carnival** celebrated in summer.

How to get organised in Oslo
To visit Oslo and take away a reasonable idea of the city you need at least three days. If this is your situation, we recommend the following plan. On the first day, visit the centre: in the morn-

ing walk along Karl-Johan avenue, visit the City Hall and the National Gallery; then make for Vigeland Park; in the afternoon, stroll through historic Christiania and the fortress of Akershus. Akker Brygge is the best place to have dinner.

Devote your second day to Bygdøy. In the morning, go to Bygdøy by the ferry that leaves from the City Hall dock. Visit the

17 May: National Day of Norway and Jazz Festival.

Vigeland Park: the Monolith.

Kon-Tiki, Fram and Viking Boats museums. At mid-day, have lunch and take a stroll through the Folk Museum. In summer these all close at 18.00 h. Go back to Oslo by bus and dine in the Karl-Johann area.

On the third day visit the ski jump at Holmenkollen and the surrounding areas. When you get back to Oslo, visit the Munch Museum.

At dusk, if you have some free time, take a cruise along the fjord and again take a stroll through the constantly changing atmosphere of Aker Brygge.

If you only have one day, there are two travel agencies who organise coach trips that take you past the points of greatest tourist interest in the city.

Perhaps that would be the most practical and convenient thing to do.

Includes is a panoramic tour around the centre, Vigeland Park, the Viking Boats Museum and the Fram in Bygdøy, and a visit to Holmenkollen.

If you want to go unaccompanied you should plan your use of public transport well so you can visit places with restricted opening hours. In the morning stroll along Karl Johan street and visit the City Hall and the rooms devoted to Munch in the National Gallery. Catch the tram for Vigeland Park. You will need between 60 and 90 minutes for this visit. Then take the number 30 bus to Bygdøy to visit the Viking Boats Museum, and then the Fram or Kon-Tiki Museums. Return to Oslo in the ferry that will leave you at the City Hall dock just beside Aker Brygge where you will have time to shop, stroll and dine in the city's most lively district.

But the cheapest (and in fact the best) way of exploring Oslo is to buy the **"Oslo Pass"** covering one, two or three days. This card provides a series of benefits, such as free public transport, free parking in municipal parking sites, and free entry to a series of museums and places of interest for tourists.

The **Tourist Guide to Oslo (Osle Guide)**, published in six languages and distributed free of charge in hotels and Tourist Information offices, contains detailed information on all points of interest in the city: timetables, entry fees, transport and agencies that organise tourist visits.

The monthly leaflet **"What's On"**, written in Norwegian and English, lists all the events happening during your stay in the city. These guides will be a great help in discovering every facet of this enchanting, international and welcoming Viking capital, from its best known to its less popular but equally fascinating aspects.

Have a happy stay!

Gardens on the site of the Akershus fortress.

CONTENTS

EDITORIAL FISA ESCUDO DE ORO, S.A.
Tel: 93 230 86 00
www.eoro.com

I.S.B.N. 978-82-7670-094-7
Printed in Spain
Legal Dep. B. 1749-2008